DREAMS & SYMBOLS

DREAMS & SYMBOLS

HOW TO UNDERSTAND
THE MEANING OF YOUR DREAMS

LUCIEN MORGAN

SMITHMARK

This edition published in 1996 by SMITHMARK Publishers, a division of U.S. Media Holdings, Inc., 16 East 32nd Street, New York, NY 10016.

SMITHMARK books are available for bulk purchase for sales promotion and premium use. For details write or call the manager of special sales, SMITHMARK Publishers, 16 East 32nd Street, New York, NY 10016; (212) 532-6600.

This book was designed and produced by Todtri Productions Limited P.O. Box 572, New York, NY 10116-0572 FAX: (212) 279-1241

Printed and bound in Singapore

Library of Congress Catalog Card Number 96-68009

ISBN 0-7651-9788-X

Author: Lucien Morgan

Publisher: Robert M. Tod
Designer and Art Director: Ron Pickless
Editor: Nicolas Wright
Typeset and DTP: Blanc Verso/UK

CONTENTS

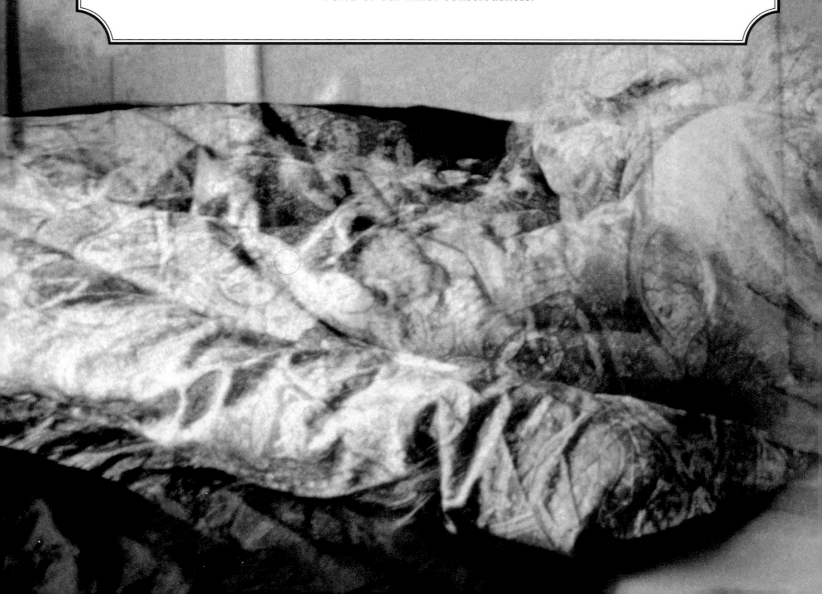

INTRODUCTION

We spend one-third of our lives asleep. And while we sleep we dream - whether we are aware of it or not. Research has shown that sleep and dreams are essential to our physical and mental well-being; even nightmares, if properly understood, can prove a beneficial experience, Freud called dreams "the royal road to the unconscious" believing them to have a hidden meaning, such as wish-fulfilment, often disguised as illusions or symbols. To him there was no such thing as a normal dream. But why do we dream ? Are our dreams really expressions of frustrated desires and failed ambitions ? And why is it that we can hardly ever recall even our most vivid dreams on awakening ? Dreams are now better understood than they were in the past, although the ancients did seem to grasp their potential in a way we can now only marvel at. The phrase "it was only a dream" no longer sounds so poignant when we realize that, with application, we can influence our dreams and explore the magical world of our inner consciousness.

SLEEP & DREAMS

ROYAL BOOK OF DREAMS AND VISIONS OF THE NIGHT.

Mortal! wouldst thou seen aright,
Dreams & Visions of the night!
Wouldst thou future secrets learn,
and the fate of Dreams discern,
Wouldst thou ope
The Curtain dark,
And thy future
fortune mark?
Try the mystic
Page, and read,
What the vision
has decreed.

The time we spend asleep is not time wasted. Nor is it a period of suspended animation, a kind of nightly hibernation. During sleep radical changes take place within both the body and mind, for while the digestive processes slow almost to nothing and the heart-rate slows down, growth hormones are released in the brain and rapidly begin their essential healing and restoring work. Recent research shows that messenger-carrying molecules are created in deep sleep, and these target individual cells in order to repair them.

During sleep the body is kept going by the autonomic nervous system, which controls the essential processes that keep us alive: digestion, heartbeat, lung function and so on. Our unconscious senses continue to be active during sleep because the brain becomes very selective and responds only to certain stimuli – for example, a mother can easily be woken by the slightest whimper from her child, although everyone else in the house will continue to sleep soundly. Most people establish their own waking/sleep routine, settling for a certain number of hours' sleep, which they more or less keep to throughout their adult lives.

Opposite: Raphael's *Royal Book of Dreams and Visions of the Night* was one of dozens of popular books to capture the imagination of the public.

Representation of an astral body, a concept believed by millions, and perhaps connected with "out of body" experiences.

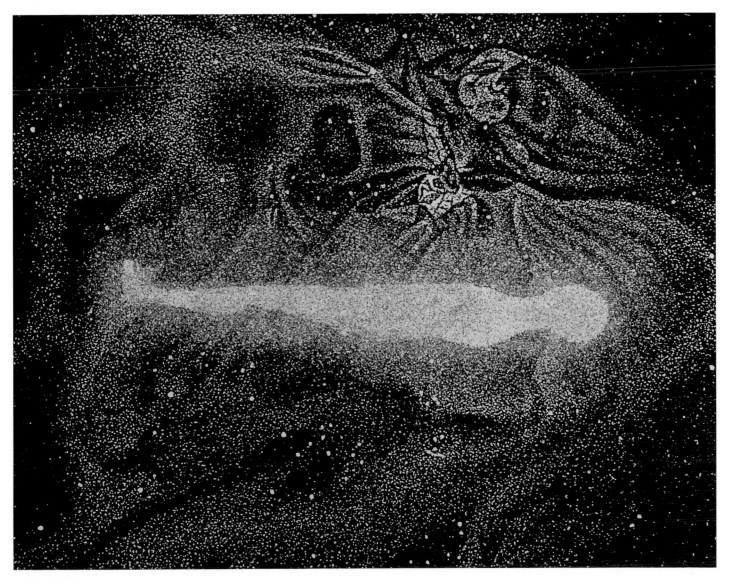

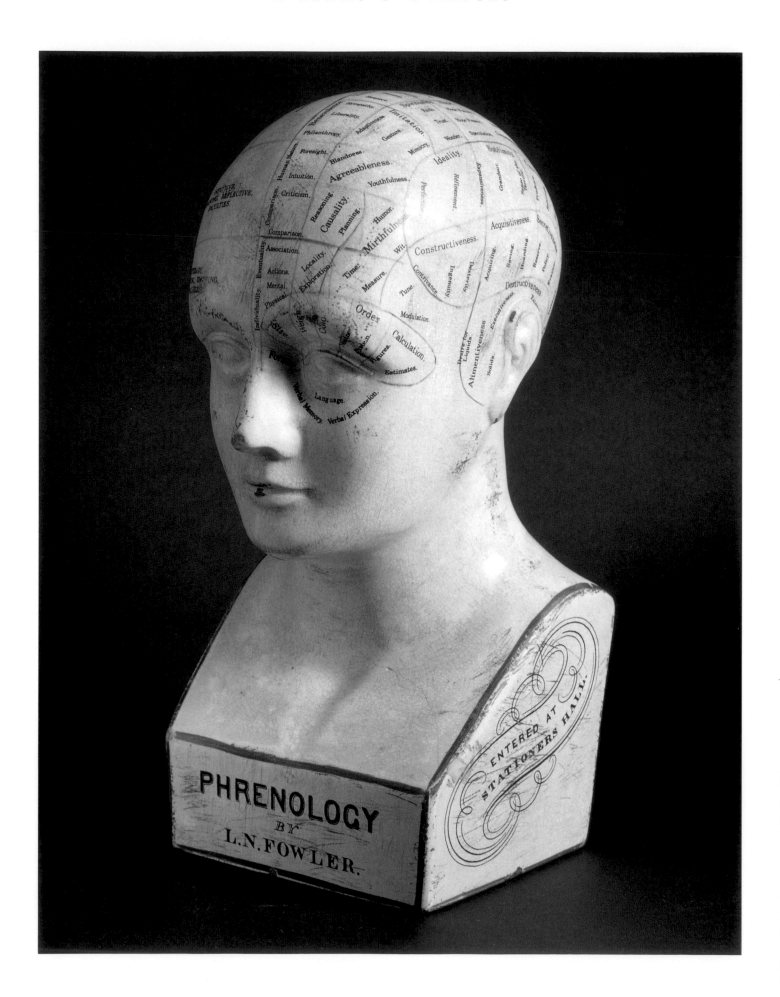

Opposite: The human mind was once thought to be simple, and phrenology (invented in 1815) divided the brain into well-defined divisions, each performing a different function.

During sleep the brain is very selective; even in deep sleep a mother can be aroused from her slumber by her baby crying — but by little else.

Scientists have discovered that it is possible to measure brain activity by observing its continual, but variable, electrical impulses. They monitor them on a machine called an electroencephalograph (EEG) – *cephalos* being Greek for "head" – via electrodes attached to different spots on the scalp. In a normal situation, before the person falls asleep, it will record a steady wave pattern known as the alpha rhythm. This is not the same as being either deeply asleep or fully awake, but represents a drowsy state. When the person falls into a deep sleep the EEG picks up delta waves, interspersed with short, fast waves, which are known as "sleep spindles". This is "orthodox sleep". Most people fluctuate from one to the other during sleep, encompassing the three main stages in ninety-minute cycles, and have on average three or four periods of big, deep-wave sleep every night.

Research has shown that the brain derives the most rest and refreshment from the earlier cycles – although the sleeper will toss and turn, changing position repeatedly. In the first hour or two of sleep the brain goes immediately into the delta phase.

During the late 1950s pioneering work by Dr Nathaniel Kleitman achieved a breakthrough in the study of sleep and dreams. He found

Dreams are rich in symbolism, much of it ill-understood.

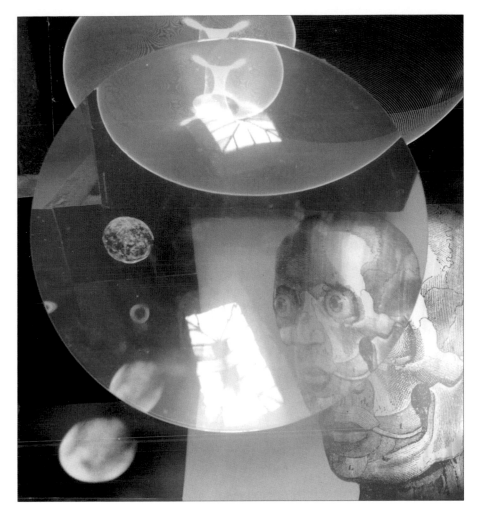

Opposite: Perhaps the quality of dreams depends on the imagination, and many of the richest have been described by artists, writers and musicians.

In dreams the rules of everyday life are waived. The laws of perspective are often ignored; sometimes the dreamer observes, sometimes participates.

that people have periods when their brainwave pattern becomes shallower and that this is accompanied by their eyes, under closed lids, moving rapidly from side to side and up and down. This is known as Rapid Eye Movement (REM) or "paradoxical" sleep, and it is the phase when people have their most vivid dreams. Their eyes are moving because they are watching their dream as if it were actually happening. This is not, however, the only period of dreaming.

Research has proved that sleep and dreams are essential for physical and mental well-being. Sleep deprivation means dream deprivation, and it is this that can bring about severe disorientation, even hallucinations, because the dreams that are being denied in the normal way are taking place during the waking state.

Exciting recent research has underlined the importance of the natural sleep rhythm of the brain/body. In the 1980s Dr Ernest Rossi made the crucial discovery that the ninety-minute cycle is actually carried on throughout normal waking consciousness. In other words, the ninety-minute cycle is repeated throughout every 24 hours and, indeed, throughout life itself. Rossi called this the "ultradian rhythm", and he has proved in his own clinical tests that making use of it is a strikingly successful way of enhancing daytime relaxation. One dramatic result is that alertness, when required, is greatly enhanced.

In his 1986 book *The Psychobiology of Mind–Body Healing* Rossi

A graphic representation of mind power, still little comprehended.

Opposite: Forms not of this world can appear in dreams alongside the utterly mundane.

explains that the best way of making use of this ninety-minute cycle is to recognize that feelings of tiredness or irritability or even the need to take a break signal a trough in this rhythm. This could well be the unconscious prompting us to rest at precisely the best time for us. If we allow ourselves to drift, we can be safe in the knowledge that the unconscious is reaping the benefit of the ultradian rhythm and finding solutions to many of our everyday problems.

FAMOUS DREAM ANALYSTS

Opposite: Sigmund Freud (1865–1939) the Austrian founder of psychoanalysis, whose *The Interpretation of Dreams* was one of the first serious attempts to apply a degree of logic to the subject.

With the rise of the Age of Enlightenment from the eighteenth century onwards, when science and industrial progress became increasingly important, dream interpretation was relegated to the realms of folklore. Nevertheless, people continued to be perplexed and disturbed by their dreams, but it was only at the end of the nineteenth century that the emergent discipline of psychology began to re-assess their value.

The most famous of that new breed is Sigmund Freud (1865–1939), the Austrian doctor who pioneered a revolutionary method of interpreting dreams. Today, there are few who totally admire his theories – indeed, there is a tendency for commentators to be increasingly hostile to his work – but it cannot be ignored because of its enormous influence within the field of psychiatry.

Freud made the assumption that psychopathology – emotional and mental problems – develops when people are consciously unaware of their true fears and motivations. They can be restored to healthy functioning when, and only when, they become conscious of what they have repressed. The focus of the therapy is to enable the patient to be aware of the unconscious conflicts that have existed in their

Do babies in the womb dream?

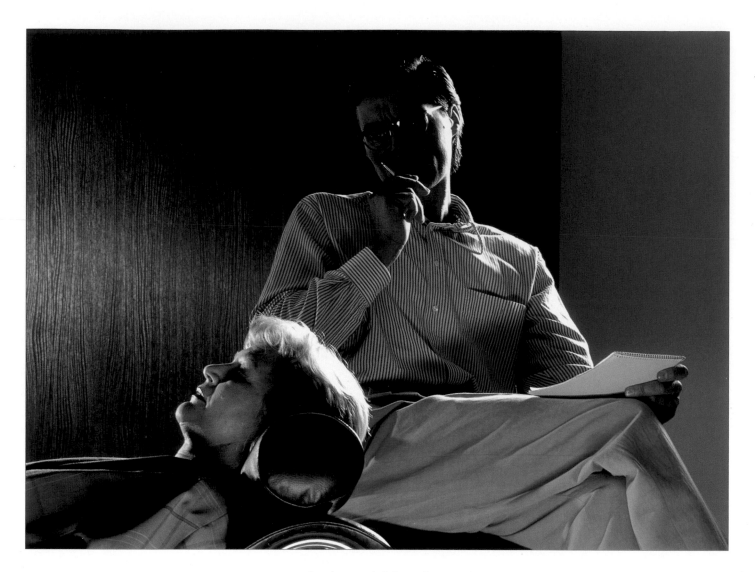

A subject undergoing analysis. A course of psychoanalysis can take many years.

Opposite: Freud divided the mind into the ego, the super-ego, and the id (the unconscious). During dreams, the unconscious comes to the fore, producing the strangest imagery.

psyche from childhood, and, by being aware of them, they can then re-evaluate them properly, at a conscious level and within the context of their own lives. For example, someone may have always hated his or her mother, but because cultural mores are against this, it was "buried" or repressed and came to cause profound emotional problems.

Freudian psychoanalysts work in a number of ways, but primarily through the use of free-association and dream analysis. For the former, the patient lies on a couch and is required to verbalize all thoughts and feelings without aiming for any coherence or structure. The analysand (patient) must try to report as accurately as possible what is going through his or her mind without screening out anything at all – including what they regard as shameful or obscene material. Freud believed that thoughts and memories occurred in associative chains and that when recent ones were reported they would ultimately trace back to those from an earlier time in the analysand's life. When memories of these childhood traumas were retrieved, the patient's ego could be healed.

Freud termed the primary conscious, deliberating, choosing portion of the personality the ego, and he considered that during sleep its defences are lowered, allowing repressed information from the

Opposite: "A Bird of Fancy en route for the evening star", a dream-like illustration by Artzybasheff from the 1927 edition of *Funnybone Alley*.

Left: The analysand often expresses him or herself in symbols to help protect the conscious mind. The image of a hand can be either threatening or comforting depending on the context.

unconscious mind to flow, although usually in a very disguised form. The analysand often expressed these in symbols to help protect the conscious mind from their true meaning. Freud termed this coding process "latent content"; "manifest content" was the dream material that he considered to be some form of compromise between the repressed information and a full expression of conscious thought.

His system of psychoanalytic therapy included theories of transference of neuroses. This came about because he had noticed that some of his patients behaved towards him in an unrealistic, emotionally charged manner, which could be positive and loving or hostile and negative. He assumed that these responses were relics of attitudes that the analysand had held towards other people earlier in his or her life and that were now being transferred to him, the analyst, as if he were one of those other people.

In 1899 Freud published his book *The Interpretation of Dreams* in which he first called dreams "the royal road to the unconscious", and like Artimidorus, he believed in the theory of opposites – that the content of dreams is really about its opposite, although, as he cannily pointed out, only sometimes. He did make it known to the public at large that dreams have a hidden meaning, usually erotic, that can, sometimes, be understood through the consultation of a stock collec-

tion of dream symbols and their meanings. He also considered some dreams to be wish-fulfilment, although the wishes may be heavily disguised as illusions, symbols or puns. For example, he claimed that rooms could represent women because he took enclosed places to symbolize the womb, which could also find expression as a cupboard or a carriage. Sharp or pointed objects, such as a dagger, pen, cigar or tower, he believed to represent the phallus and therefore to symbolize men. To Freud, there was no such thing as a straightfor-wardly literal dream.

In his book *On Dreams* the later dream researcher and playwright, William Archer (1856–1924), criticized the Freudian school on the grounds that it was possible to argue "from almost any 'manifest content' to almost any 'latent content' that may suit your purpose".

Late twentieth-century commentators, while eagerly pointing out Freud's mistaken theories, also seize on the fact of his cocaine addiction, which is unlikely to have made for the most clear-headed conclusions.

Within the fields of psychology and psychiatry, Carl Gustav Jung (1875–1961) is undoubtedly as highly regarded as Freud, and Jung's

Opposite:Carl Gustav Jung (1875–1961), a former disciple of Freud, who took psycho-analysis along more arcane mystical paths.

Sharp unrealistic perspective is a characteris-tic of many dreams, pursued to the full by the Surrealist painters such as Dali and Chirico.

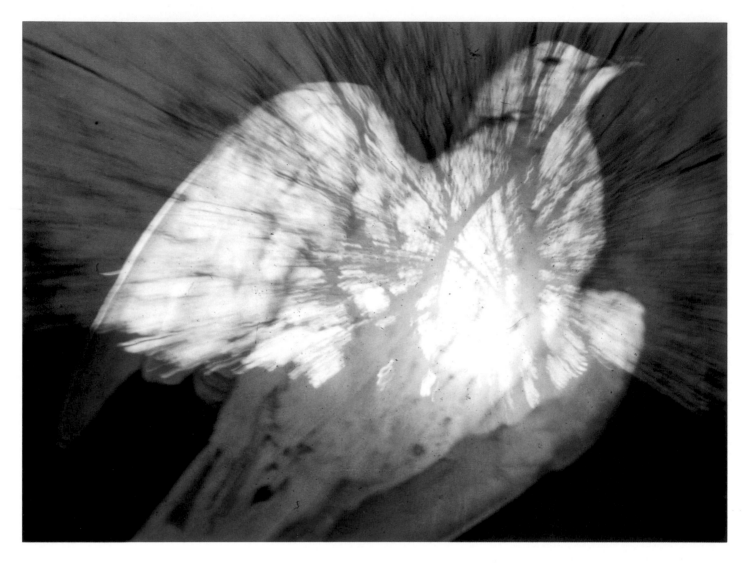

Dreams, Jung believed, could give expression to any kind of mental, emotional or spiritual potential, and uncovered mankind's pool of shared dream images which he terms the collective unconscious.

Opposite: The Egyptians put great store in dreams, perhaps because they saw in them inklings of the after-life in which they so much believed.

theories are still fashionable, especially in New Age circles. Jung's dream theory diverged from Freud's because he felt that the Freudian approach was too constricting. Dreams, he believed, could give expression to any kind of mental, emotional or spiritual potential – including telepathy. Jung's work was remarkable for its emphasis on the alleged paranormal and mystical content of dreams.

In particular, Jung believed he had uncovered mankind's pool of shared dream images – the archetypes – for example, the hermit-like, wise old man. Such symbolic figures are most usually found in the imagery of the classic Tarot decks. But although Jung first published his ideas in *Modern Man in Search of A Soul* in 1933, it was not until 1984 that his theories were first systematized. In *Understanding Dreams* Mary Ann Mattoon clarifies his theory of dream interpretation by listing his four tests for the validity of his analysis:

1 Does the interpretation "click" with the dreamer?
2 Does the interpretation "act" for the dreamer?
3 Is the interpretation confirmed (or not dis-confirmed) by subsequent dreams?
4 Do the events anticipated by the interpretation occur in the dreamer's waking life?

The essence of this is that patients in Jungian analysis must grasp the significance of their dreams and take whatever appropriate action appears to be dictated by them.

However, there is one vastly underrated analyst without whom no overview of this subject would be complete. This is the virtually unknown Captain W.H.R. Rivers (1864–1922), a British doctor in the Royal Army Medical Corps during World War I and, in his day, a noted anthropologist.

During the conflict of the Great War Rivers became convinced of the efficacy of dream interpretation in the healing of such mental scars as were suffered by shell-shock cases, although as he pointed out "the psychology of dreams was not deemed worthy of inclusion in a course of academic psychology" when he was a medical student. The volte-face that had since taken place was, in his opinion, entirely due to the influence of Sigmund Freud. However, Rivers was no admirer of that doctor's method or theory. He considered them to be unscientific and so arbitrary as to be useless. Specifically, he disagreed

Above and opposite: Images of war often feature in the dreams of soldiers or ex-soldiers. Captain W.H.R. Rivers (1864–1922) was convinced of the efficacy of dream interpretation in the healing of shell shock.

with Freud's notions of dream opposites and with his view that latent content in dreams was disguised by our unconscious mind so that it would not shock our conscious selves.

Rivers argued that the dreams employ disguises because dreaming is actually a very primitive process. He accepted that dreams contain dramatizations, symbols and residues of information picked up during the day: what dreams do, he suggested, is to confront us with the difficulties we face in our waking life, but in dream terms.

At Craiglockhart mental hospital, where he treated shell-shock cases – including the poet Siegfried Sassoon – in 1917, Rivers discovered the value of nightmare. He noticed that men fresh from the hell of the trenches had atrocious nightmares, accompanied by screaming and excessive sweating, but as they recovered, the bad dreams and all their side effects lessened in intensity. Rivers noted that children are particularly prone to nightmares because they do not have access to more sophisticated ways of dealing with their problems – the recurring nightmare is a sure sign that problems are not being dealt with, whereas their lessening indicates that a successful solution has been found.

Dreams, Rivers believed, represented an evolutionary expedient, yet unfortunately their very essential childishness is what discourages most people from bothering to analyse their dreams. His own experience had reinforced the idea that dreams contain extremely valuable,

Opposite: Men fresh from the hell of the trenches in World War I often suffered from the most appalling nightmares, but with sympathetic treatment these usually faded with time.

Strong contrasts of light and shade are a basic element of dreams.

and often practical, advice about a host of problems, if only one can learn how to unlock their meanings – which can be very direct if one takes them seriously.

While both Freud and Jung had the benefits of money and the backing of a large publishing house, besides veritable armies of admiring neurotics who clung to their every word, Rivers had none of these. He was a hard-working doctor who, sadly, died while he was still in his fifties, before his book *Conflict and Dreams* could be revised. However, he made an appearance in Siegfried Sassoon's autobiography, *Sherston's Progress*, as "that great and good man". Perhaps his wisdom and kindness were due in part to his previous travels among the peoples of the South Seas, particularly the shamans or *kahunas* who routinely use dreams when dealing with sick or disturbed people.

These days it is generally recognized that analysands frequently react to their particular analyst by reporting the kind of dreams they think they want to hear about. For example, the patient of a Jungian therapist will dream in archetypes, and that of a Freudian analyst will

Even the amiable cat can be transformed in the dream state into something unutterably terrifying, while a bird in flight (below) expresses freedom.

39

Opposite: A skull smoking a cigarette, perhaps reflecting the uneasiness of the dreamer.

There are no rules in dreams. A girl with a plant bathed in blue fluorescence may be difficult to interpret, but she would be in some kind of context, perhaps forgotten when the dreamer woke up.

report dreams abounding in imagery such as sharp objects.

Dreams can be put to active use in many ways in therapy. In my own hypnotherapy practice clients are encouraged to treat the dream state as an alternative, but very safe, reality: for example, people who are using hypnosis in order to give up smoking may not smoke in their everyday existence, but they can smoke in their dreams. Sexual fantasies can also be experimented with in dreams safely and without embarrassment.

The evidence is that dreams are a much under-used human resource: they can clarify our underlying problems and motivations, they can reveal our true feelings about others, they can take the pressure off present predicaments – and they can even be used for recreational purposes, if programmed by hypnotic suggestion and understood in the right way.

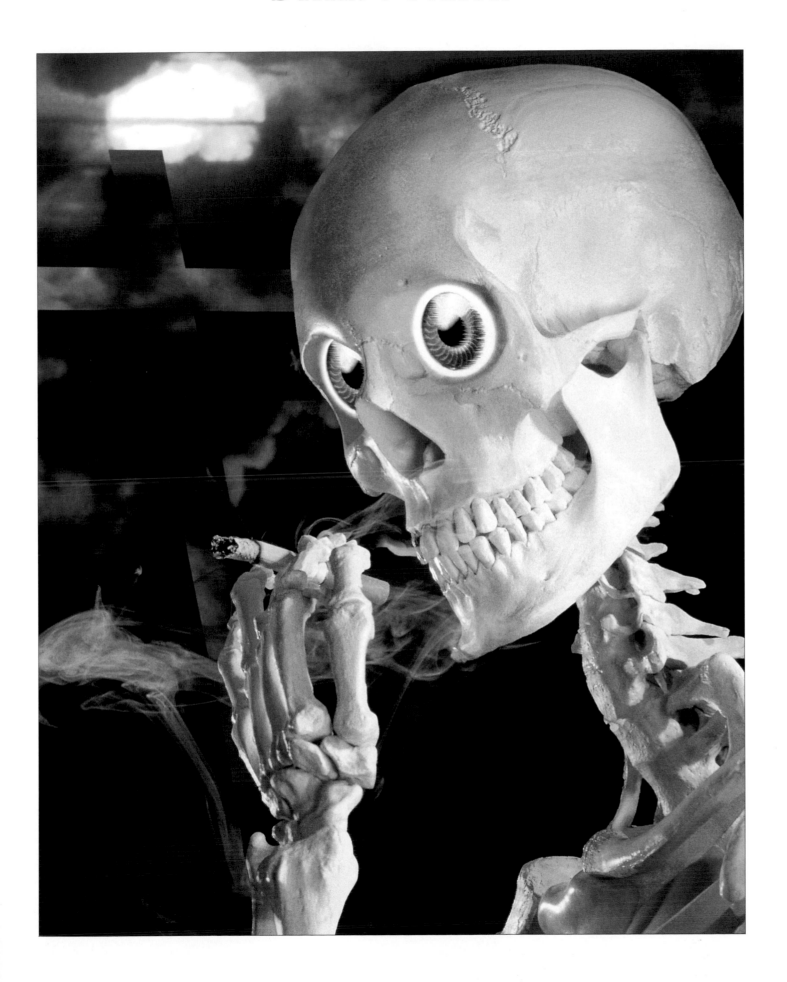

Nightmares & How to Cope With Them

*F*rom time to time most people suffer from nightmares, but some have them repeatedly – recurring nightmares. Whatever their frequency, they do seem to be a natural part of the human condition.

The most commonly shared nightmares take the form of being pursued (sometimes by a monster), being confronted by some menacing or paranormal figure, falling, being in a terrifying or normally life-threatening situation such as a house-fire, or being tortured or even killed. Some social or business scenarios can be turned into nightmares, such as being found out in a lie or being told off by an authority figure in a humiliating manner.

Some people suffer terribly from abnormally frequent and/or

Opposite: The incubus and succubus, imp-like demons, were once believed to have sexual intercourse with men and women during sleep. They were particularly active during the years when witchcraft flourished.

A man with glowing eyes, a daunting image, but not uncommon in dreams.

intense nightmares, often to such an extent that they feel their whole lives are wrecked and they dare not go to sleep. In rare cases the nightmare is so vivid and realistic that the dreamer finds it hard to shake off, so that virtually the whole of their lives becomes tinged with terror.

However, it is a mistake to over-exaggerate the power of nightmare over the average person. And it is possible to learn, not only how to cope with the occasional nightmare as it arises, but also to benefit positively from the experience it offers.

The clue to the conundrum of nightmares lies in the fact that children suffer from them much more than adults. As dream researcher W.H.R. Rivers pointed out, nightmares suffered by adults indicate that they reflect emotions or emotion-charged situations that the dreamer is not mature enough to deal with in other ways, so they surface in these exceptionally bad dreams.

The content of some traumatic dreams can be "fixed" – established in the unconscious – during childhood. For example, dreams of falling or fear of heights can be the direct result of something as simple as the child having slipped in its mother's arms while being bathed as a baby. This innocuous event, which was not even noticed by the mother at the time – perhaps too much soap made the infant temporarily hard to hold – was registered deep within its psyche as a primitive terror. The experience and excessive fear of falling then

Opposite: Portrait of the occultist, poet and novelist Howard Phillips Lovecraft (1890–1937) with his monstrous creations, the picture by David Carson. Other poets, such as Coleridge with *Kubla Khan*, have delved into their dreams and imagination with more benevolent results.

Overleaf: Some traumatic experiences can be fixed in the unconscious during childhood — even a visit to the zoo and seeing some strange frightening creature, and subsequently amplified in the dream state.

Of all the activities in dreams, there is nothing more common than free-falling, though it can be a pleasurable experience.

manifests in later life as a nightmare, which perhaps recurs. Echoes of this will also be felt in waking life as a fear of heights.

The connectionist theory seeks to explain how the brain conditions us into responding in a specific and repeated way to memories of past trauma. Despite what many non-scientists believe, no one has ever located the part of the brain that deals with memory. What we think of as deeply ingrained memory seems in reality to be continually re-created in the brain. At large festivals, such as the opening ceremonies of the Olympic Games, there are often highly trained people who are choreographed to present at the same instant one particular side of the square card they carry, and then present, simultaneously, the other side. This simple manoeuvre has the stunning effect of creating in a second one large colourful picture, then with another single movement, the next – completely different – picture. Similarly, the brain – out of habit – creates and perpetuates even the most apparently ingrained and bad "memories". In this author's view, it may do this because the brain knows it has survived a very bad experience, and is replaying that event actually to reassure itself that it is possible to do so. So such dreams do not, in fact, represent – as most people think – a kind of masochistic reliving of dreadful past events, but are

Hand-coloured engraving by William Blake (1757–1827) to Blair's graphic and eerie poem *The Grave* (1812).

Opposite: Dream-images can be merged, perhaps a device to avoid a rational explanation when the dreamer awakes.

instead a form of reminiscence about a triumph.

    Nightmares may also allow us to experiment with our reactions to different horrific scenarios, or to rid ourselves of the extreme emotion that may be, as it were, accumulating as we go through a life that is particularly mundane. The ancient Greeks believed that people enjoyed going to the theatre and watching tragedies – complete with the usual quota of murders and mutilations – because of catharsis. This is the idea that by seeing such tragedies and horrors being enacted, the playgoer is cleansed of the profound emotions of "pity and terror" and therefore leaves the play drained but emotionally balanced. Another, more recent view on watching dramatic enactments of such horrors, comes from the screen-writing authority, Julian Friedman. He believes that people go to see films at an unconscious level in order to rehearse for the most extreme experiences in real life. So the car chase, the explosion, the sex attack or whatever else one sees in a movie is showing the cinema-goer what could happen to them and is allowing them to prefigure their response to a similar situation. Friedman also observes that the brain reacts to the drama on the screen by releasing a powerful "excitement" chemical that creates an instant natural "high" – as if the person has actually survived the crisis themselves. Of course not all screen characters have the unnatural longevity of James Bond, but even when the screen characters do not survive, the audience has still had the benefit of having absorbed

Nightmares may allow us to experiment with our reactions to unpleasant scenarios, or even to speculate "what would happen if ...?" Prehistoric creatures in a city street may not be likely, but one never knows ...

Opposite: Bad dreams do not necessarily represent a kind of masochistic reliving of past events, but are instead a form of reminiscence about a triumph.

Opposite: The owl, symbol of wisdom for thousands of years, and to dreamers wholly benevolent (unless they happen to be mice!)

Skulls are a convenient metaphor for death. In earlier days when most people died before they were forty, the skull was an everyday symbol of time passing, and it did not have the macabre overtones of today. Their presence in dreams may not necessarily be threatening.

the possibility of encountering that particular scenario.

Dream horrors are said by some to be aspects of our own personality that are personified as, or symbolized by, the attacking animals, rapists or catastrophes or any of the terrifying figures that people our nightmares. For example, a woman who dreams that her mother is threatening her may feel appalled and guilty because her mother is a kind and loving woman who would never do such a thing in real life. But the dream may in fact represent the dreamer's own maternal side, which she could feel threatened by in some way.

Nightmares can also arise because the unconscious has picked up subliminal clues about deeply hidden anxieties and is exaggerating them in the form of nightmare in order to bring them to the dreamer's attention. In this way nightmares can be positive because they bring to the fore matters that would otherwise remain unnoticed and unresolved. For example, a nightmare of teeth falling out is classically interpreted as financial insecurity but could also mean that your teeth need immediate attention, possibly for something as simple as a filling. The longer the dreamer ignores the message of the nightmare the more vivid – and even violent – it will become.

Such academic insights may be of small comfort to the sufferer, but there are proven methods of coping effectively with nightmares:

1 Find out what the symbols are within your nightmare. Fritz Perls, the creator of Gestalt therapy, utilized the technique whereby one addresses an empty chair in which one visualizes the dream enemy sitting. Talk to it and ask it who it is, where it is from, what it represents and what it wants. This may sound bizarre, but you can gain a surprising amount of essential information in this way. After all, you may "only" be visualizing this scenario in your mind, but that is precisely where your dream enemy came from in the first place.

2 A quite separate technique is based on the idea that the unconscious will find its own way of coping with nightmares if you ask for its help. While it is true that it is just as much part of you as your conscious self, for the purpose of this exercise it is useful to think of it as a separate being. Indeed, an effective part of this technique is to give your unconscious its own name, which you keep secret. Use a simple form of self-hypnosis – counting down from ten to zero – and tell your unconscious that you are about to enter a beautiful trance that will dissolve into a deep, healing sleep that is nightmare-free. This trance state is not sleep, but it enables you to access the unconscious much more easily than when normally awake. Only give yourself positive, beneficial suggestions when in this trance state. Whatever you suggest will be acted upon by the unconscious. It is important to remember, before you enter the trance, to give yourself the suggestion that, if an emergency should arise, you will come out of it completely and immediately. Under no circumstance practise any form of hypnosis while driving a car or operating machinery.

3 If your nightmares involve a harsh, cruel or nagging voice, it is possible to change it into something that sounds much more pleasant. Do this by imagining it as being much more seductive and visualize the accompanying scene as being more to your liking.

4 Learn how to control the nightmare by employing the technique of lucid dreaming (see next chapter).

5 Prevent nightmares by making positive changes to your lifestyle. It is important to give up alcohol, get physically fit and develop your sense of humour. It may be a well-worn phrase but it is true that in this case at least, laughter really can be the best medicine. You may also benefit from taking up an activity such as sport or dancing.

6 Modern technology is available to help people overcome their nightmares. Tuvi Orbach, the London-based Israeli businessman, has developed a highly sensitive bio-feedback machine, Relax Plus. Simply by attaching electrodes to the fingertips and becoming increasingly relaxed you can see the extent of your relaxation in the form of a computer animation. This begins as a small swimming fish, and if you relax successfully it gradually changes into a mermaid, a girl on land, an angel and then a star. Tension or a failure to maintain your relaxed state means that the visual images run backwards, ending with the static fish.

Nightmare sufferers have shown that, by thinking of their nightmare at the same time as using the machine and watching the animation

Opposite: Melting watches is the main feature of one of Salvador Dali's best-known paintings, illustrating the impermanence of time.

Overleaf: A professional hypnotist at work. Hypnosis was one of Freud's main methods, easily achieved, as is self-hypnosis.

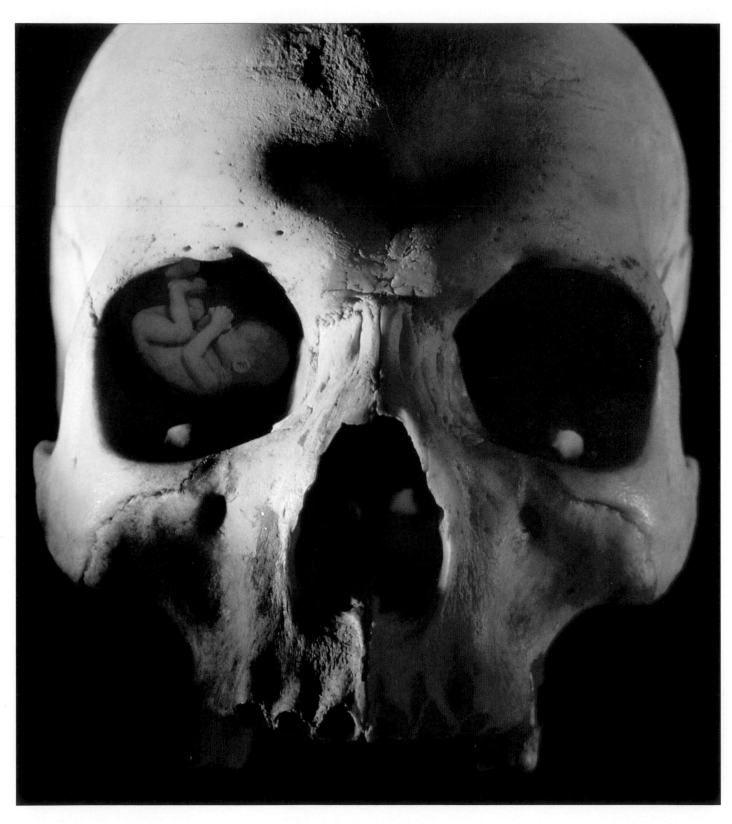

An embryo in the eye-socket of a skull, symbolizing the close connection between death and rebirth, only realised under analysis.

Opposite: Adam's Dream of Lilith by Fay Pomerance.

they can make the dream images into something much less frightening and gain control over them.

The single most important thing to remember about nightmares is that they are not random horrors. They always have a reason and it is always one that profoundly concerns you. Learn to deal with them and they can provide a potent key to self-realization.

DREAMS THAT COME TRUE

Opposite: The dream of Charlemagne the Great (742–814) in which the king is saved from a bear and a leopard by a hound. The illustration comes from Andrew Lang's *Book of Romance* (1902).

Semi-transparent figures feature in many dreams, with often a mixture of utter realism and total fantasy.

As the flames roared and shot higher, she somehow realized that this was a royal palace – and it was being destroyed by fire. When the grandmother from Humberside awoke she knew that her dream would come true, because she had experienced many such dreams. Sure enough, three weeks later, Barbara Garwell saw on the television news that the chapel of Windsor Castle had burnt down – exactly as she had seen it. She, it seems, "specializes" in precognitive dreams (those that come true), but many people have had one or two such dreams in their lives.

More tragic is the story of nine-year-old Eryl Mai Jones who, on 21 October 1966, told her mother about a terrible dream in which she had gone to school but it was not there. "Something black had come down over it," she said. The dream had been so disturbing that she was reluctant to go to school, but her mother told her it was "only a dream" and so she went. In the event, she was one of the 140 teachers and children who were killed when half a million tons of coal waste slid down onto the little Welsh school at Aberfan.

Another warning voice came in the form of a dream for Balkan Bishop Monsignor Joseph de Lanyi during the night of 27 June 1914.

Opposite: Many authorities on dreams believe that dreams can foretell the future, and there is certainly ample documentary evidence to support this view, as there is of the ability of fortune-tellers to make true predictions.

In it he saw on his desk a black-edged letter which bore the arms of his one-time pupil, the heir presumptive to the Austro-Hungarian throne, the Archduke Ferdinand. When he opened the letter a scene unfolded. He saw the Archduke in a car with his wife, facing a general. Two men suddenly fired at the royal couple. The letter read:

Your Eminence, dear Dr Lanyi, my wife and I have been victims of a political crime at Sarajevo. We commend ourselves to your prayers. Sarajevo, 28 June 1914. 4 a.m.

The next day the Bishop heard of the assassination. And shortly afterwards, the whole of Europe was at war.

It is impossible to say exactly what proportion of people experience premonitory dreams because many of them are no doubt afraid of being laughed at if they make them public. Fear of ridicule lay behind the unfortunate reticence of one John Williams, a Cornish tin mine manager, who had a disturbing and vivid dream twice in May 1812. Later he wrote:

Some dream visions have no connection with anything on land or sea, and may be similar to the "heightened consciousness" experienced by those who use hallucinatory drugs.

I dreamed that I was in the lobby of the House of Commons. … A small man dressed in a blue coat and white waistcoat, entered, and immediately I saw a person whom I observed … dressed in a snuff-coloured coat with metal buttons, take a pistol from under his coat, and present it at the little man above-mentioned. The pistol was discharged, and the ball entered under the left breast of the person at whom it was directed. I saw the blood issue from the place where the ball had struck him, his countenance instantly altered, and he fell to the ground. Upon inquiry who the sufferer might be, I was informed that he was the chancellor. I understood him to be Mr Perceval, who was Chancellor of the Exchequer.

(In fact, Perceval was also Prime Minister.) When the shaken Williams described the dream to his wife, she, too, said it was "just a dream". But when he went back to sleep that night he had exactly the same dream. It was only a few days afterwards that Perceval was assassinated – exactly as in Williams's two dreams.

One world leader who had a dream premonition of his own untimely death was Abraham Lincoln, who told his friend Ward Lamont a few days before his assassination:

Opposite: Trees in a mist with a naked figure. Dreams are frequently erotic, and Freud's view that such dreams are clothed in complicated symbolism no longer holds, though it may have done when he was writing a century ago.

A marvellous bat-like creature from nightmare, originally created by the great French graphic artist Gustave Doré and reshaped by the eccentric English cartoonist George Cruikshank.

There seemed to be a death-like stillness about me. Then I heard stifled sobs, as if a number of people were weeping. I thought I left my bed and wandered downstairs. There the silence was broken by the same pitiful sobbing, but the mourners were invisible. I went from room to room; no living person was in sight, but the same mournful sounds of distress met me as I passed along ... I was puzzled and alarmed. What could be the meaning of this? ... I kept on until I arrived in the East Room, which I entered. There I met with a sickening surprise. Before me was a catafalque, on which rested a corpse wrapped in funeral vestments. Around it were stationed soldiers ... there was a throng of people, some gazing mournfully upon the corpse, whose face was covered ... "Who is dead in the White House?" I demanded of one of the soldiers. "The President," was his answer; "he was killed by an assassin!" Then came a loud burst of grief from the crowd, which awoke me from my dream. I slept no more that night; and although it was only a dream, I have been strangely annoyed by it ever since.

Dream-images do not have to have logic. Here is a face made up of clouds. It may be that imaginative people have the more imaginative dreams.

Opposite: Endlessly travelling to no-one knows where is a common characteristic of dreams, and may represent the dreamers' real-life dilemmas.

Overleaf: The sea in dreams does not usually mean drowning, and is often a soothing feature, sometimes but by no means always associated with birth.

71

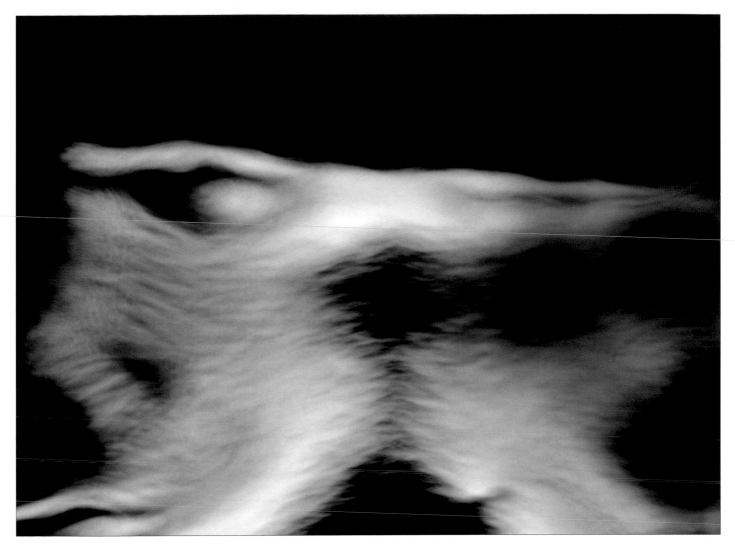

Most of the world's greatest dramas or most pivotal events have been prefigured in dreams. But some that involve public figures do not always happen exactly as in the dream. For example, one that has been quoted by Professor W.H. Tenhaeff of the University of Utrecht, Holland, was reported to him by a patient who had unusual dreams. After promising to keep him updated with them, she described one in which she:

> Saw a railway crossing and a long road and pasture. Behind the gate to the left stood a truck. A car comes along at a terrible speed trying to cross at the last moment but as it crosses, a tyre bursts and the car crashes at full speed against the gate and the truck behind it. The driver of the car was killed immediately. I saw his face when he was lying there. It was Prince Bernhard [of the Netherlands].

Two days after this was reported to Tenhaeff he heard that Prince Bernhard had indeed been involved in such an accident beside a railway track. But there was no railway crossing, no burst tyre – and, most significantly of all, no death. For although the Prince had been

Many people believe that they leave their earthly body during sleep, emerging as an astral figure which is free of all normal constraints.

Opposite: Such an image would no doubt be incomprehensible to the dreamer on waking up, but it may be amenable to analysis and less obscure than it first appears.

Opposite: Such is the pace of progress that real-life photographs, which would have been scoffed at fifty years ago, now have the quality of dream-images.

Overleaf: A crusted and distorted clock. This may be a hint to the dreamer that it is time to wake up, and so wonderful are the ways of the unconscious mind that such a nudge will be promptly acted upon.

The bird of prey is often seen in the world of dreams, perhaps an equivalent to an underlying menace the conscious mind does not want to face.

thrown onto the road by the impact of the collision with the truck, he survived.

Not all precognitive dreams concern public figures or even particularly significant events. British author J.B. Priestley described how a BBC sound engineer dreamed that a sparrow-hawk perched on his shoulders. The dream was so vivid that he actually felt its claws. Just two hours later, when he was in the living room of his lodgings, his landlord came in to throw some junk on the fire. It included a stuffed sparrow-hawk, which one of his fellow lodgers picked up and stuck on his shoulder "and dug its claws into the shoulder of my jacket with sufficient force to enable it to remain standing on my shoulder". Obviously he felt its claws, just as in the dream.

There are many such apparently pointless precognitive dreams on record – some of which only predate the event by minutes, even seconds. A common one is a dream that you wake up and switch on the light, which immediately "blows" – and this happens. Another such dream is where you are looking at the clock and note that it is say, 6.20 a.m. Then as you are looking at it, the ticking stops. Then you wake up and it happens exactly in this way.

Opposite: There is no question that abstract painters and artists of the Symbolist school show dream-like influences in their pictures, especially recapturing the mood of many dreams.

A young girl dreaming, from a photograph by the French photographer C. Puyo dating from about 1908.

Sometimes dreams that appear to be precognitive may simply be the result of the dreamer having unconsciously picked up signals or clues beforehand. For example, a young woman, whose boyfriend was just about to go on a cruise, dreamed that she went on board to see him off, but discovered him there with another woman, who turned and laughed cruelly at her. When she awoke, it was as if she was under a massive black cloud of depression and "stone-cold certainty that the dream had something important to tell me. I knew he had lied to me about going on the ship by himself." A brief, and extremely emotional telephone call soon ascertained the truth: her boyfriend was going to travel with another woman. But in this case there may not have been an authentic paranormal element involved: she may have picked up clues from his behaviour at an unconscious level, and her dream then transformed them into a graphic drama. However, this dreamer now believes that she can tell the difference between dreams that present the literal, or near-literal, truth about a coming event, and the usual fantasies. "There is a special feeling that goes with dreams like this," she says. "When you wake up there is an

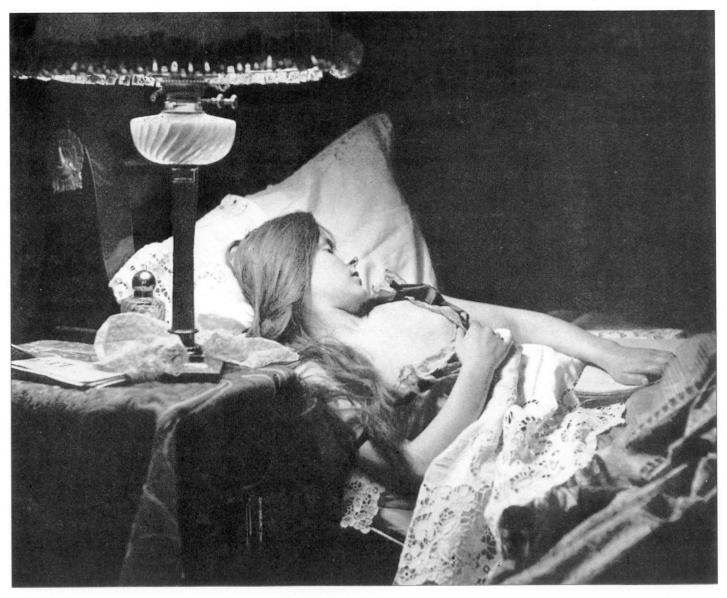

A journey into the great unknown. Dreams can propose solutions to our problems, and without dreams it is difficult to say what mankind would have become. As a third of our life is spent in sleep, it is a major part of everyone's life.

Opposite: "Embryonic form moving into the plane of being on a ray of coloured light" The content and culture of dream is often taken up by arcane and mystical cults.

immediate, absolute certainty such as you never normally feel about anything else. I put this down to the sheer power of the unconscious hammering through."

Happy events of the future can, and often do, first make themselves known to us in our dreams. One woman dreamed she was frantically shopping for a fancy hat, although she was "not normally a hat person at all", and felt curiously happy when she finally bought "one of those joke Australian bush-hats with the corks hanging off all the way round". She woke laughing at the apparently ludicrous dream, but within hours her daughter had telephoned and announced, completely unexpectedly, that she was engaged to be married – to an Australian.

The question is not whether dreams can predict the future, for the evidence seems to point that they can, but whether our unconscious minds have continuous access to past, present and future or whether this happens only occasionally.

Although premonitory dreams can be about any kind of event – tragic, personal, or happy – perhaps the more dramatic it is the more we tend to remember it. And of course dreams about catastrophes are the most spectacular, so it could be that they tend to be reported

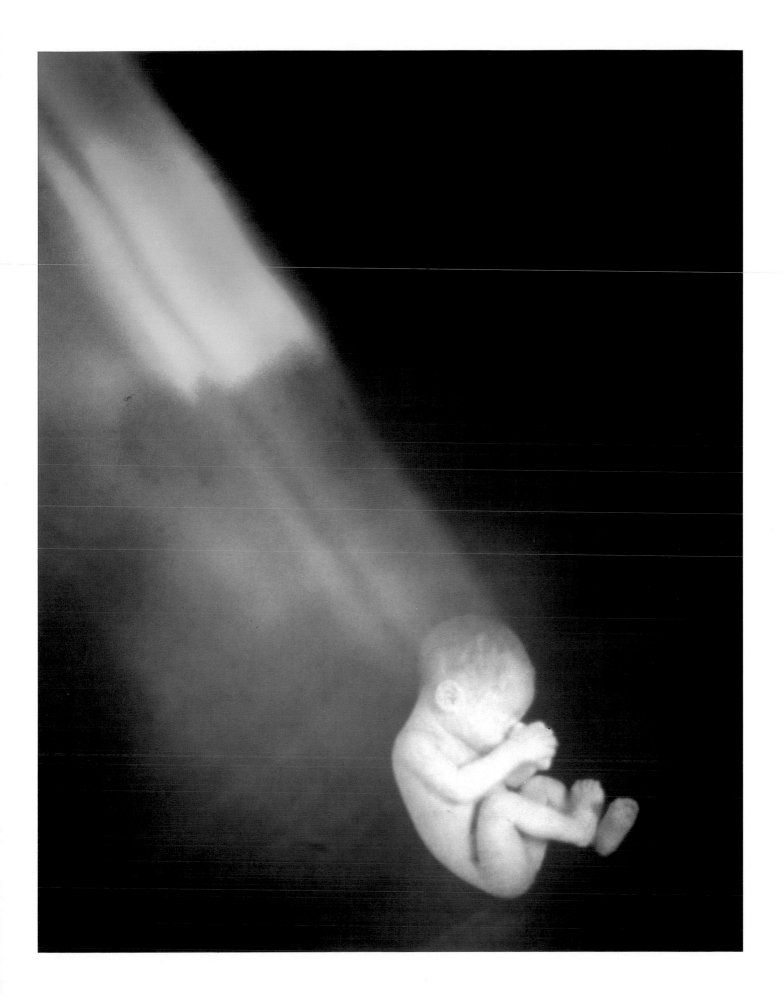

Opposite: Many authors, such as Graham Greene, have related how significant their dreams were to them. An image from one of his childhood dreams was to remain with him for more than sixty years.

most often. However, Professor Ian Stevenson of the University of Virginia, who has researched this subject for decades, believes that the more calamitous the episode, the more likely it is that people will pick it up by telepathy.

British author Graham Greene describes how important dreams have been to him in In a Sort of Life:

> On the April night of the Titanic disaster, when I was five and it was Easter holiday time in Littlehampton, I dreamt of a shipwreck. One image of the dream has remained with me for more than sixty years: a man in oilskins bent double beside a companion-way under the blow of a great wave. Again in 1921 I wrote home from my psychoanalyst's: "A night or two ago I had a shipwreck dream, the ship I was on going down in the Irish Sea. I didn't think anything about it … it was not until yesterday, looking at an old paper, I saw about the sinking of the Rowan in the Irish Sea. I looked at my dream diary and found that my dream had been Saturday night. The accident had happened just after Saturday midnight." Again in 1944 I dreamed of a V1 missile some weeks before the first attack. It passed horizontally across the sky flaming at the tail in the very form it was to take.

Dreams enable the dreamer to indulge in fantasy, free from reproof or misunderstanding. Dreams are essentially private property.

Opposite: The awesome and destructive power of a volcano was never more apparent than the eruption of Krakatoa — as predicted in a journalist's dream.

The laws of nature are suspended during dreams. The various themes are incorporated into narratives, and if weightlessness is involved even gravity is totally ignored, or, on the contrary, gravity can be exaggerated during "escape" sequences so that the dreamer seems to be pinned down.

Sometimes, however, the most well-worn stories about dream messages that are apparently about future events can turn out to be very disappointing. On 29 August 1883, for example, Edward Samson, night news editor of the *Boston Globe*, woke from a vivid nightmare. In it he had witnessed a massive volcanic eruption on an island near Java: many people were burnt to death as the whole land mass blew apart. Samson had been sleeping on a couch in his office due to a very alcoholic evening, and when he staggered off home the next day his scribbled notes on the dream, which he vaguely thought might come in useful for a short story one day, were misunderstood as being a late news story by the incoming day editor. The *Globe* rushed into print with what it thought was a scoop about a major disaster, only to cringe with embarrassment when the truth came out that evening.

Samson was sacked, but within hours cables began arriving that told of the eruption of Krakatoa – and its destruction seemed to have happened at the very time of Samson's dream. But was it really a prediction? In fact, the *Globe's* front page story about Krakatoa was based on a cabled item sent from London the day before, not a dream. And the newspaper never

John Wilkinson

Opposite: Many natural features have dream-like overtones, due to their innate mystery, quietness, and remoteness, as do enigmatic man-made structures such as the dolmens of Ireland and the standing stones of Wiltshire, in England.

Some symbols can be self-evident, such as a key.

even had an editor named Samson …

The fact remains, however, that many genuine dreams of a precognitive nature are recorded, but nothing is quite as exciting as experiencing such dreams oneself, for then one's preconceptions about time and the very nature of reality come into question. I myself have had many dreams that came true, although few were quite so dramatic – nor, in retrospect, so hilarious – as the one I had in 1978 when I was working for a medieval jousting tournament on tour in Britain.

Sleeping in the horsebox, I dreamed that I was galloping at great speed on the nearby Doncaster racecourse. Everything about it was vivid and immediate. I was woken by a colleague with the news that the horses had escaped in the night and we had better recover them swiftly. Eventually we recaptured all eight of them at the other end of the racecourse and decided to ride them back bareback, using only their halters to steer. Every one of them proceeded to bolt in a kind of mass frenzy – and it was only when we had careered halfway towards the winning post that my dream came back to me …

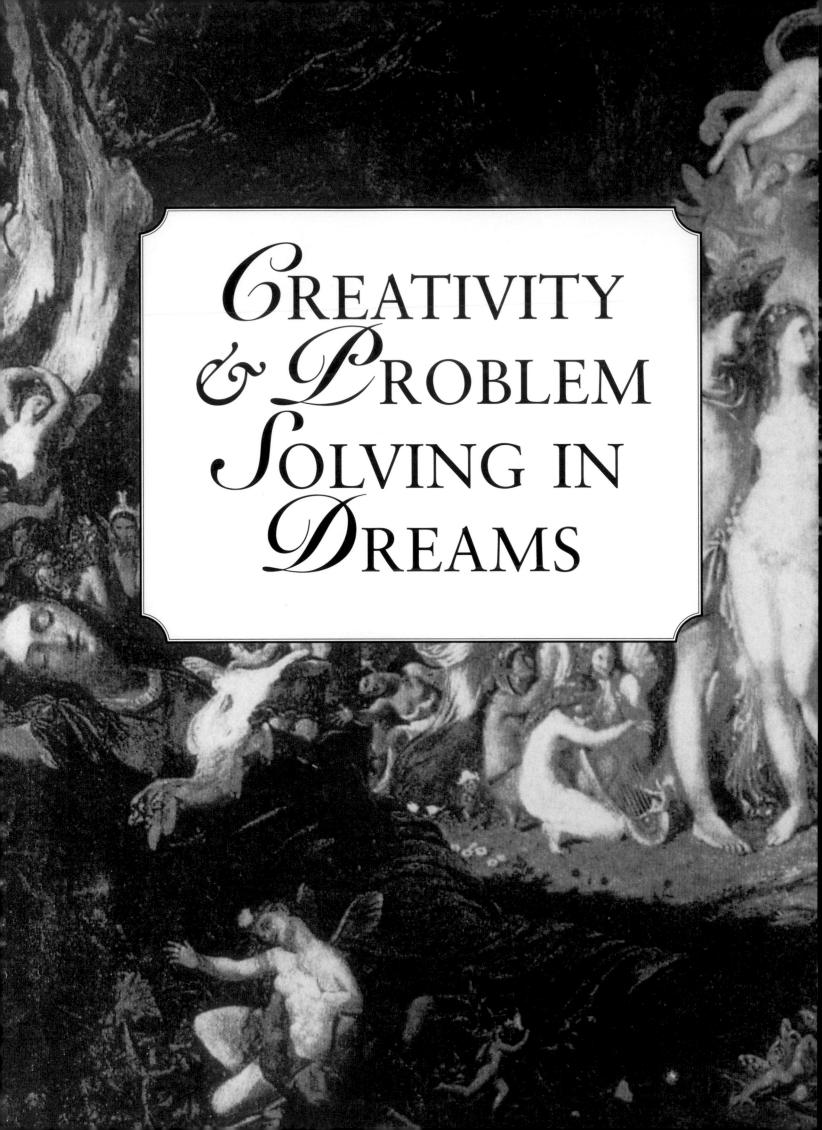

CREATIVITY & PROBLEM SOLVING IN DREAMS

Opposite: Dreams are vast reservoirs of untapped creative potential, and workaday problems can be solved during sleep.

Dreams are vast reservoirs of untapped creative potential, and it is during those vital night hours that many of our apparently most intractable problems are sorted out by a profound unconscious process. The old idea of "sleeping on" a problem and waking up with the solution clearly in our minds is based on the experience of generations – and is reinforced by modern research.

Many famous exponents of different arts and sciences have almost come to rely upon the gift of dream creativity. Perhaps the greatest of all was Leonardo da Vinci (1452–1519), the Florentine whose genius extended to visualising the helicopter, the sewing machine and even the bicycle. Despite his incredible productivity, it is well known that he spent the same amount of time asleep as he did awake, and that he also induced trance states during his waking life in order to solve problems. Perhaps his use of altered states of consciousness allowed him greater vision and aided his already considerable powers of lateral thinking.

The writer Robert Louis Stevenson says in his *Across the Plains* (1892):

"The illusion never lasted long", an illustration by Artzybasheff from the 1927 edition of *Funnybone Alley*, an apt comment about dreams. Dreams should always be written down on waking before they can be rationalised.

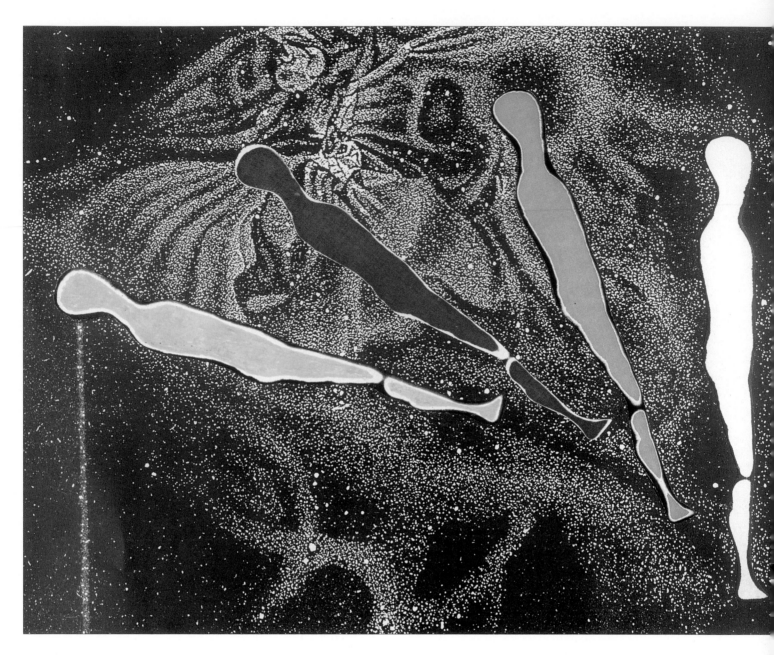

A diagram illustrating astral travel, showing the stages in the liberation of the astral body from the earth plane, according to the description given by Sylvan Muldoon in about 1923.

Opposite: "I'd be very, very lonely sitting up here all alone", an illustration by Artzybasheff from the 1927 edition of *Funnybone Alley.* The conversations and dialogues in dreams are often elaborate and intricate, but, more than the visual aspects, which are often universal, these relate to the specific individual. A dreamer can only think of what he or she knows in real life.

There are those among us who claim to have lived longer and more richly than their neighbours; when they lay asleep they were still active; and among the treasures of memory that all men review for their amusement, these count in no second place the harvest of their dreams.

Stevenson himself was able to contact his unconscious mind in order to "harvest" ideas for his stories, and personified the dream creatures who gave him them as "Brownies". They were particularly fond of passion and the picturesque in fiction; in fact, he claimed they gave him the plot of the dark drama of Dr Jekyll and Mr Hyde.

Other novelists who owe their characters or situations to dreams include Jack Kerouac, the American beat poet, J.B. Priestley, the British writer who was obsessed with the concept of time, Sir Walter Scott and Graham Greene. But one of the most famous writers in this category is surely Charles Dickens, who came to rely on his afternoon naps in order to further his plots and who said that

The Dream of Life by Andrea Orcagna (c. 1308–68), who created a hieratic art in which gold backgrounds played an important part. In medieval times there was less distinction between fact and fantasy and in many ways people then lived in a kind of dreamworld.

George Relph, was an actor of extraordinary charisma seldom put to greater effect than in William Archer's 1923 play *The Green Goddess*.

Right: A strange other-worldly rendering of elements from Shakespeare's *A Midsummer Night Dream*.

Opposite: Representation of the myth of Gaea, the earth goddess, holding aloft the lunar satellite Selene. Dreams formed an

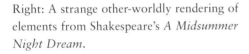

during these naps new characters appeared to come and stand before him in the flesh.

It was during the Victorian era that organizations of ceremonial magic were fashionable among theatricals: the Order of the Golden Dawn boasted among its members Bram Stoker, author of Dracula, and the Irish playwright, poet and mystic, W.B. Yeats. The latter acknowledged a wealth of creative input from his dreams, which he wove into all his work.

It was J.B. Priestley who actually dreamed the basic plot of his famous play *Time and the Conways* (1937), and William Archer's play *The Green Goddess* (first performed 1923), which did excellent business on both sides of the Atlantic, sprang from his dreams. Archer, a journalist, had become fascinated with dreams and with Freud's analytical process in particular, and he had meticulously recorded all his own dreams as a result. The play revolved around the story of a Raj (played with extraordinary power by George Relph) who exploited the magic of an idol.

One of the most famous of all stories concerning creativity in dreams is that of Samuel Taylor Coleridge (1772–1834), the

Opposite: An illustration depicting a Sunday afternoon in Lincoln Park, inspired by Georges Seurat (1859–91), whose pointillist techniques and cool sharp imagery have a detachment and stillness wholly dream-like.

Romantic poet and friend of William and Dorothy Wordsworth, feverishly scribbling down the poem that had come to him complete in an afternoon nap when a "man from Porlock" came to visit and the rest of the poem evaporated from his mind. We know the fragment as the fantastical, perhaps even magical "Kubla Khan".

Magical too, were the works of the German writer Johann Wolfgang von Goethe (1749–1832), whose own interest in mysticism almost certainly aided his output. But magical training is not, as millions of ordinary people will attest, necessary in order to seize the extraordinary inspiration that is offered in dreams.

Time and time again in my screen-writing seminars I have met dozens of hopefuls who confess that a "writer's block" seems to spell the end of an otherwise promising project. This is the moment to call on the unlimited inspiration of the unconscious: I teach them how to gain access to their dreams through a self-hypnosis technique that can often explode a block for ever. The key to this inner world is lucid dreaming, which will be discussed in detail later. Briefly, however, that is where the sleeper knows he or she is dreaming and can learn to control, even radically change, the dream scenario. This can enable an otherwise fluently creative person to eliminate temporary "blocks"

Painting *The Three-fold Sleep in Eden* by Fay Pomerance.

A young boy on the beach surrounded by objects he would have discovered there. Early memories often surface in disguised forms in dreams, often with powerful emotional overtones.

and set out the development of character and plot – just as Charles Dickens actually dreamed a great deal of his novels. It is the unconscious that does the work.

Whenever the development of other characters and development of scenarios are called for, the dreams can be of enormous help. As I have found with student actors learning the "method", when the need to "become" someone quite different from their normal selves is paramount, learning to use dreams produces impressive results in addition to teaching them more about themselves. The final characterization is often much more real, more "organic", because it actually came from inside themselves rather than being imposed artificially from outside.

Masters of the visual arts have often acknowledged dreams as sources of their inspiration; one of the most famous of these was the late eighteenth-century British poet, painter and mystic, William Blake.

Many of his poems owed much to dream input – witness the deceptive, almost child-like simplicity of:

Tyger! tyger! burning bright
In the forests of the night,
What immortal hand or eye
Could frame thy fearful Symmetry?

Opposite: Mesmerism and animal magnetism were names given to hypnotism in the early years, widely satirised, and often used in association with simple electricity—giving mild electric shocks to a circle of people.

Paul Gauguin celebrated the beauty of the South Seas in several paintings, one of which, The Spirit of the Dead Watching (1892), came directly from dream inspiration.

But of all schools of art, it was the coming of the Surrealist Movement that best encompassed the strange world of dreams. Its founder, André Breton, wrote in the Movement's 1924 Manifesto that its aim was "to reconcile the contradiction which has hitherto existed between dream and reality in an absolute reality, in a super-reality".

Many musicians have dreamed large tracts of what was to become their most poignant and compelling pieces. Mozart, Beethoven, Vivaldi and Wagner all recognized that some of their genius, while still resolutely their own, came from that part of their minds that blossomed during dreams.

Much nearer to our own day, one particular songwriter woke with a piece of music so complete in his mind that he was convinced he had heard it somewhere and was merely remembering it. For days he played it to musician friends asking them if they knew what it was, to no avail. In the end he had to acknowledge that he had actually written it in his dream. He went on to record it and it is now one of the most famous pieces of music on earth. He is Paul McCartney, and the song was "Yesterday".

One of the characteristics of dreams is that the dreamer can only bring into his sleeping hours personal experience and knowledge. Even dreams of precognition would be set out with these boundaries in mind. A grand piano in a misty setting could feature in the dreams of a musician, but hardly likely in the dreams of a shepherd.

Delaying the Ageing Process

DELAYING THE AGEING PROCESS

Growing old appears to be an unavoidable fact of life. No matter how many expensive health spas we attend, vitamins we take or beauty treatments we indulge in, it seems inevitable that our minds and bodies degenerate only too swiftly and distressingly on the way to the grave. There is evidence, however, that this "inevitability" is merely the result of centuries-long conditioning. We see wrinkled old people hobbling along with their walking frames and unconsciously begin to imitate them by gradually degenerating ourselves in a similar way. We seem to be complying with an unwritten rule, as if in obedience to a bigger, more omnipotent presence. Whether that presence is what we take to be God or whether it is society at large, we act unconsciously to maintain what is in effect a consensus reality. But the fact is that we have all been brainwashed into believing what is not necessarily true – mankind has the option of at least delaying the ageing process significantly, not through the use of wonder drugs or potions, but by using something we all have already. This is the secret power of our dreams.

The central concept of this revolutionary technique is that of "time anchors", which this author developed using his own experiences and those gleaned from his therapeutic practice. Briefly, the way to delay

Opposite: A young child's face interspersed with flowers. Many feel embarrassed by the inconsequential, as some do by the erotic — the dreams of John Ruskin, the great Victorian art critic, drove him mad. They were, he said, disgusting.

When religious beliefs were strongly held, angels were key participants in dreams, as is evident from recorded accounts, but unquestionably they have been replaced by more contemporary symbols.

Man and time, two great mysteries. Growing old appears to be an unavoidable fact of life, but perhaps the apparent inevitability is due to conditioning.

the ageing process using this method is to choose a day in the past when you were the happiest you have ever been. As before, use the self-hypnosis technique by counting down from ten to zero then visualize a golden light around your body, and "see" your chosen scene intensely. Recall everything, from the way you were dressed, sights, scents, feelings and the event itself. The olfactory sense (our sense of smell) goes directly to the brain, which is why an unexpected scent can bring back such powerful associations and why aromatherapy is so successful.

Visualize within the scene a golden anchor, perhaps lying against a wall, and from it emanates a golden chain that is attached to the light around your body. Imagine the thoughts, feelings and sensations that you felt at the time coming back to you now. This simple exercise is most effective if done every night immediately before going to sleep. You can ensure that the visualization is carried on into your dreams simply by giving yourself a post-hypnotic suggestion to that effect as soon as you have created the scene. The visualization and the subsequent dream will act together and your body will quickly begin to respond to them by producing the same chemicals it produced at the time when the scene originally happened – perhaps when you were fifteen years old. During the next day you will react by feeling full of life and vitality.

110

This works because the mind activates special messenger-carrying molecules that mimic the chemical circumstances you experienced on the original day you had such a "high".

Young people can pre-empt the ageing process by visualizing themselves in the future, for example, dancing the night away or scuba-diving at the age of ninety five years.
The golden anchor and chain will naturally draw the person intensely into this mental vision of their future selves, and help to ensure that it comes about. This will then be reinforced by the dream that you subsequently drift into.

Recreational lucid dreaming is also a highly effective way of delaying the ageing process. Once you have control of the content and process of your dreams you can make them present you with the scenario of your choice – and if that happens to be yourself as young, beautiful and healthy at a ripe old age, so much the better.

Being aware of Rossi's ultradian rhythm – the endless ninety-minute cycle – will also help us to maximize our potential, by keeping us aware of the very best times in which to rest and relax. In this way we will be in tune with our natural rhythm and have more energy when required and more rest when it is needed, with the end result that we benefit from the optimum powers of physical and mental restoration that are available to us.

Dreams are often a means to return to youth. Youth, it has been said, is wasted on the young.

INTERPRETING DREAMS

There are many books about dream interpretation, and, as we have seen, very different schools of thought about how to approach the subject: the Freudians, with their emphasis on repressed eroticism, the Jungian school with its more mystical and cosmological tendency, and many others. But while it is true that dreams communicate in their own style and "language", the most important factor is that they emanate from the individual's own psyche and ultimately, therefore, can be comprehensively understood only when seen in the context of the dreamer's life as a whole.

The world of dreams can seem as intrinsically perplexing as a foreign country and its method of communication just as impenetrable as another language. However, the heartening fact is that the basic rules of this language are considerably easier to grasp and to apply than those of, for example, Spanish or German. Once the key is learned, the rest follows automatically.

The main points to remember in dream interpretation are that most of the major schools of dream analysis are correct – but only partially. They undeniably contain useful insights and strategies for understanding the dream code, but their intransigence makes them too inflexible when dealing with, for example, dreams that arise from many cultures or under specifically personal circumstances. Adherents of a particular school of interpretation tend to induce in

Opposite: A sharp cryptic image, perhaps denoting envy, the desire for a better car which is unattainable, reflected by the bird cage in which the car is imprisoned.

The world of dreams can be seen as intrinsically perplexing as a foreign country and its method of communication just as impenetrable as another language.

their analysands the very kind of dream that their system promotes. For example, a Jungian analyst will find that his or her analysands will describe dreams full of archetypes and mystical imagery. This does not, however, imply – as it might seem at first – that the Jungian system is in some way the best or the only one that works. Be aware that although all these systems are undoubtedly useful, they are only systems.

Professional dream analysis is not necessary. Most people can learn to interpret their own dreams, perhaps having recourse to the literature or enlisting a friend's help from time to time. Dream interpretation is, however, a discipline like any other form of study of intensive hobby. It calls for dedication and commitment, and true understanding of your dreams will only come with time, study, thought and experience.

A dream diary is essential: keep a tape recorder or pencil and notepad by your bed and make a record of your dreams every morning without fail even if you can only remember fragments, or if your dream seems nonsensical or pornographic. This record is for your eyes only, and it may well prove invaluable – and the actual words you use will provide highly relevant clues as to the meaning of the dream, especially in punning or symbolic content.

Above: A turn of the century treatment of dream imagery.

Serpents are essentially associated with sex.

Opposite: One of the curious ambiguous images of dreams, in which a naked woman is projected against an Egyptian head.

"A Song of Sleep" by Walford Graham Robertson (1867–1948) for his play *A Masque of May Morning* (1904). Robertson was one of the talented group of artists and illustrators who flourished in London in the 1890s.

The mood of the dream is exceptionally telling. You may have dreamed a scenario that otherwise would seem tragic or happy, but if your feelings on waking are the opposite, then the actual message of the dream needs to be examined very carefully. Always make a note of how you feel after your dreams.

Dreams are widely perceived as being so confusing because they are a mixture of literal and symbolic material, and they often take the form of enactments of puns.

Literal material is frequently composed of jumbled memories of the day's events, and quasi-literal dreams can take the form of re-working past events, as in classic anxiety dreams – for example, repeatedly going over sitting an examination but discovering you do not know what the subject is. Literal dreams can also convey important and direct messages. For example, a dream of visiting the dentist may simply mean that it is high time you went for a check-up, or that your unconscious had picked up early signs of trouble with your teeth that you had no knowledge of at a conscious level.

The symbolic content is what usually makes dreams seem so perplexing. It can make the dream scenario seem so ridiculous as to be deemed utterly useless. It is, however, extremely important and should never be ignored. Often it takes the form of puns, plays on words that become little scenes, just as in the game of charades. For

Opposite: Dreams in which the dreamer finds no way out are common, and dreams incorporating mazes can be quite disturbing — there is a way out but it can't be found.

If you are worried about money you may dream about swimming and finding yourself out of your depth. Or alternatively you could simply just dream about bank-notes.

example, if you are worried about money you may dream about swimming and finding yourself out of your depth but then find that someone helps you keep afloat. In the circumstances this is a dream to cherish, because the message is that you are aware, at an unconscious level, that someone will help you out.

Puns are only one kind of dream symbol that need to be understood before attempting to interpret your dreams. According to some schools of thought, all symbolic content represents aspects of the dreamer's own self, and while this may be a sweeping statement, it does seem to be true as far as certain symbols are concerned. For example, a house symbolizes the dreamer's whole self, and the various rooms stand for different parts of his or her personality – the attic is the higher mind, the bedrooms are sexuality, the kitchen is nourishment and emotions, the library the store of knowledge, the hall represents the comings and goings of people and events, the basement is the deep unconscious, and the bathroom is where guilt is washed away or kept private. Similarly, the furniture used in dream houses contains its own valuable codes. For example, a dress in a trunk in a basement could refer to happy times spent in the distant past.

The most exciting aspect of doing your own dream interpretation is that, given dedication and the commitment of time and study, you will build up a stock of symbols that are your own. Your personal

Windmills would have no definite interpretation put upon them, not being one of the archetypal dream images, and their significance would depend on the context.

religious beliefs, for instance, may find a unique expression in your dreams, and after a while you will become familiar with their nuances – yet you will not find these symbols in any book about dreams. They are your very own.

Your own ideas about dream interpretation will, as we have already noted, influence what kind of dreams you have. Your unconscious will provide you with material that fits in with your school of thought and give you the symbols that you will find easiest to interpret.

External influences should never be discounted. The belief that eating cheese for supper gives rise to all vivid dreams may be very largely an old wives' tale, but it is true that diet does play an important role in helping to create our dreams. Going to bed hungry can make for a disturbed sleep, and waking up during the night will usually mean that you remember the dreams from which you have just woken, giving the impression of unusually vivid dreams. Similarly, too much alcohol, although it can induce deep sleep at the beginning of the night, will then go on to cause broken sleep and dreams, often with a nightmarish quality that is hard to shake off on waking.

Environment is important, too – everything from the type of bed you sleep on to the phases of the moon have been cited by

researchers as significant factors in creating the quality of the dreams we experience. Some people are particularly sensitive to beds other than their own, and holidays can be ruined by a hotel's mattresses.

There are, however, tried-and-tested techniques that can alleviate these problems. Self-hypnosis, for example, is a proven method of inducing deep, restful sleep and of allowing the unconscious to communicate fluently through dreams. Some researchers advise you to visualize a deep golden energy field around you to induce a profound sense of comfort and relaxation.

It is only too easy, in this as in all matters, to be blinded by science. It is important to remember that the mind and brain are very largely uncharted territories and no one knows all the answers.

As we enter the new millennium we are coming into very exciting times: not only are all aspects of the fields of neurology and psychology being increasingly researched but it is also becoming clear that many non-scientists have profoundly wise insights to offer, and we are in the process of recovering the best of the ancients' knowledge. Just a hundred years ago people boasted that soon they would know everything there was to know. Now we recognize that the sum of human knowledge has an unlimited horizon.

While the conquest and exploration of outer space will no doubt

Some researchers advise you to vizualise a deep golden energy field around you to induce comfort and relaxation. Equally, emerging from the dark into the light has much the same therapeutic effect.

Opposite: It is important to remember that the mind and the brain are very largely uncharted territories and no one knows all the answers.

One of the saddest phrases in the world is "it was only a dream", thus relegating an entire magical kingdom to oblivion.

provide us with more information and questions to answer, there will be a greater emphasis on working with the equally uncharted world of inner space. And it is here that dreams will finally be seen as the essential key to wisdom and self-realization that brings happiness.

The important thing, however, is to enjoy your dream life. Becoming too serious or obsessed about it will induce an artificial neuroses, and will result in dreams to match. It is essential to forget everything about dream analysis every few months in order to maintain a balanced and healthy approach to the subject. Dream and enjoy …

> You could not reach
> the ends of the psyche
> though you went the whole
> way; so deep is its nature
> *Heraclitus, c.500 bc*

One of the saddest phrases in the world is "it was only a dream", thus relegating an entire magical kingdom to oblivion. Dreams are only beginning to be properly understood, although the ancients did have an enviable grasp of their potential for conveying urgent messages to the dreamer. It may well be that dream research – the exploration of inner space – will assume a greater importance than that of outer space.

To quote singer-songwriter Deborah Harry, "dreaming is free". Yet it manages to give us entertainment, advice, healing, excitement, insight and unlimited potential – besides offering a means to delay the ageing process.

INDEX

PICTURE CREDITS